John Harbison

THE FLIGHT INTO EGYPT

for four-part chorus of mixed voices
with soprano and baritone solos
and orchestra accompaniment

Winner of the 1987 Pulitzer Prize in Music

G. SCHIRMER, Inc.

DISTRIBUTED BY

HAL•LEONARD®
CORPORATION

7777 W. BLUEMOUND RD. P.O. BOX 13819 MILWAUKEE, WI 53213

JOHN HARBISON

John Harbison was born in Orange, New Jersey, in 1938. He studied at Harvard College and Princeton University before joining the faculty of the Massachusetts Institute of Technology in 1969. He is the first permanent holder of the Class of 1949 Professorship at MIT. From 1982 to 1984, at the request of André Previn, he was composer-in-residence with the Pittsburgh Symphony Orchestra, and held the same position at the Los Angeles Philharmonic, continuing his association with Previn.

Harbison has received commissions from the Koussevitzky, Fromm, Naumburg, and Rockefeller foundations, as well as from many performing organizations, including anniversary commissions for the Boston Symphony (100th), New Haven Symphony (90th), and San Francisco Symphony (75th). His music has been performed by such organizations as the Aspen and Berkshire festivals, the San Francisco Opera, the New Opera Company (England), the New York Philharmonic, and the Fires of London. Recordings of Harbison's music are available on Nonesuch, CRI, and New World.

Also active as a conductor, Harbison has been music director of the Cantata Singers (1969-73, 1980-82) and co-director of the music ensemble, Collage (from 1984). He has conducted many orchestral and chamber ensembles, including the San Francisco, Boston, and Pittsburgh symphonies, Speculum Musicae, and the Boston Symphony Chamber Players. Many of his works have been given their premieres by Harbison's wife, the violinist Rose Mary Harbison.

Harbison's cantata, *The Flight into Egypt* received the Pulitzer Prize for music in 1987.

Commissioned by the Cantata Singers
David Hoose, Music Director

The Flight Into Egypt

**For Four-Part Chorus of Mixed Voices
with Soprano and Baritone Solos
and Orchestra accompaniment ***

Matthew III, 13-23 KJV

John Harbison (1986)

Moderato (♩=88)

* Orchestral score and parts are available on rental from the publisher.

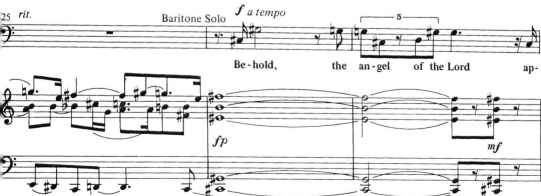

Baritone Solo

Be - hold,   the an - gel   of the Lord   ap-

4

pear - eth ___ to Jo - seph in a dream, say - ing:

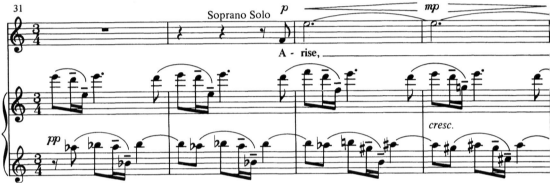

Soprano Solo

A - rise, ___

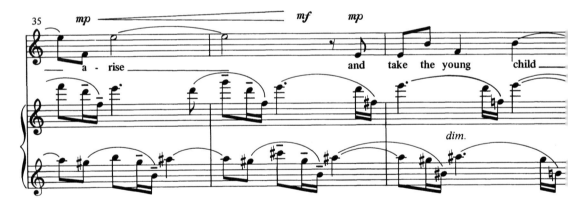

___ a - rise ___ and take the young child ___

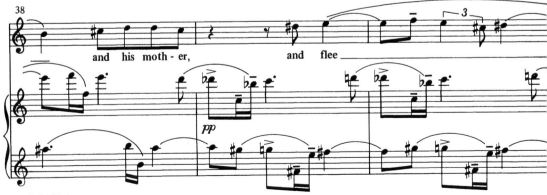

and his moth - er, and flee ___

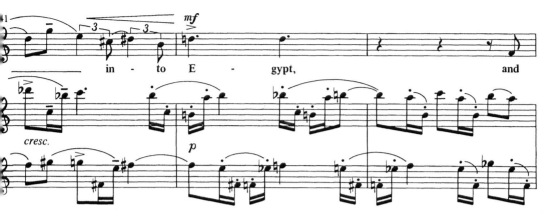

into E - gypt, and

be thou there un - til I bring thee word, _____

for He - rod will seek the young child to de -

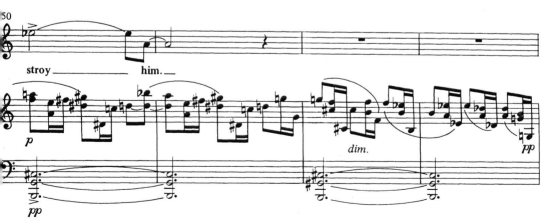

stroy _____ him. _____

6

Baritone Solo

When he a-rose, he took the young child

and his moth-er by night,

and de-part-ed in-to E - gypt:

And was there un-til the death of He-rod: ___

that it may be ful-filled ___ which was spok-en of the Lord ___

___ by the proph-et, say - ing:

8

Mosso ♩ = 132

110 *rit.*

113

116

119 Baritone
Solo

Then   He - rod   when he saw that he was mocked   of the wise   men,

AMP 7978-3

was ex - ceed - ing wroth, and sent forth, and

slew all ___ the chil - dren that were in Beth - le - hem and in

all the coasts there - of; ___ from two years old and

un - der ac - cord-ing to the time which he had dil - i - gent-ly en-quired of the

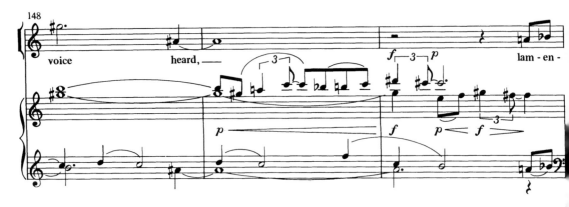

voice heard, — lam - en -

ta - tion and weep - ing

and great mourn - ing.

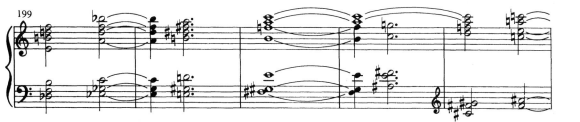

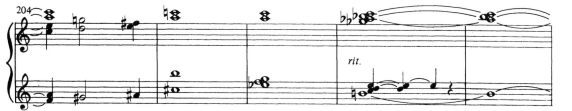

Tempo I ♩ = 88

209 Baritone Solo

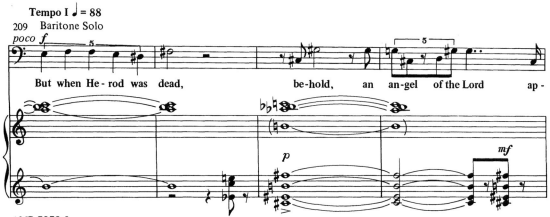

But when He - rod was dead, be-hold, an an-gel of the Lord ap -

pear - eth _ in a dream to Jo - seph in E - gypt, say - ing,

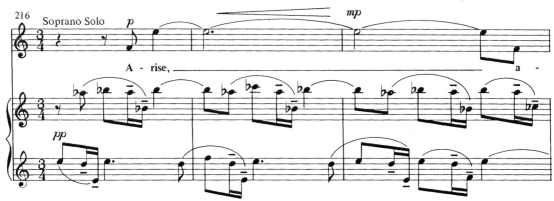

Soprano Solo

A - rise, _____ a -

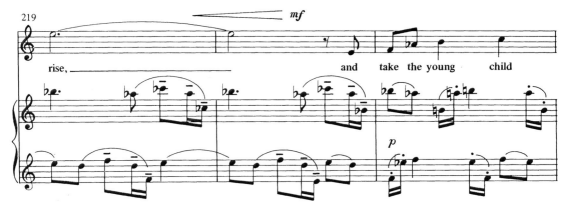

rise, _____ and take the young child

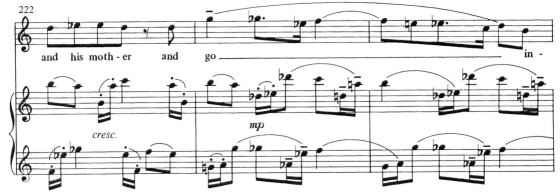

and his moth - er and go _____ in -

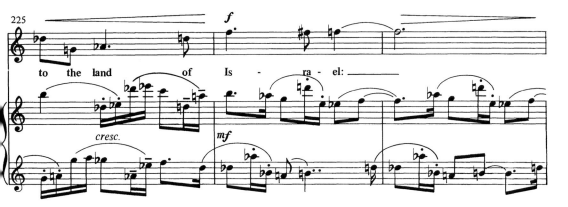

to the land of Is - ra - el: _____

for they are dead which sought _____ the young child's _____

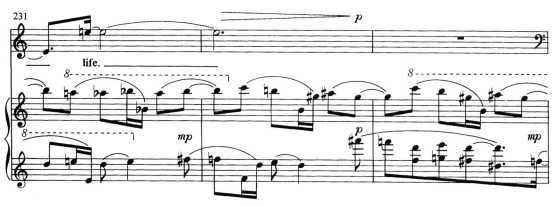

life. _____

Baritone
Solo

And he a - rose _____ and took the

poco stacc.

young child _____ and his moth - er, _____

and came in - to the land of

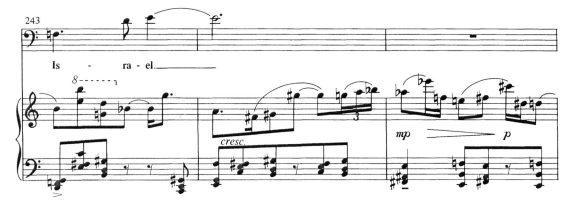

Is - ra - el. _____

24

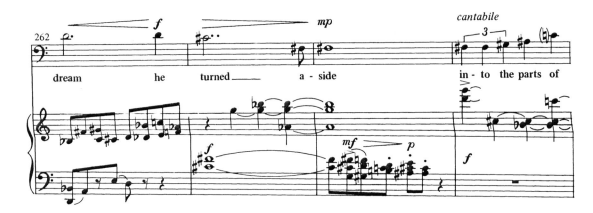

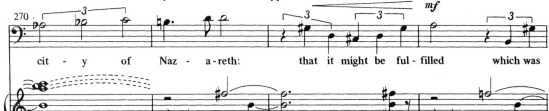

AMP 7978-3

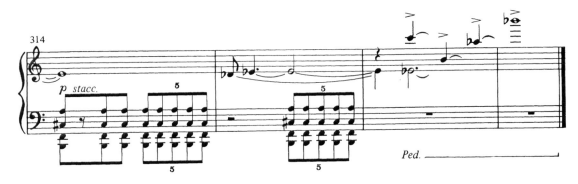

AMP 7978-3

Token Creek, Cambridge, 1986.